MY MOTHER'S GENTLE UNBECOMING
THE ABSENTINGS OF ALZHEIMER'S

LINES FROM THE SIDELINES

DAN WETMORE

ISBN-13: 978-0999787328
ISBN-10: 0999787322

UNIVERSITY
P R E S S

St. Andrews University Press

St. Andrews University
(A Branch of Webber International University)
1700 Dogwood Mile
Laurinburg, NC 28352
press@sa.edu
(910) 277-5310

Editorial Board

Paul Baldasare
Joseph Bathanti
Richard Blanco
Betsy Dendy
Robert Hopkins
Edna Ann Loftus
Madge McKeithen
Ted Wojtasik

Ted Wojtasik, Editor

Ronald H. Bayes, Founding Editor
1969

I believe the printed word benefits from a soundtrack as much as do moving images, and that the following will complement the reading as much as - if not more than - they aided the writing.

Sorrow is Shadow Cast by Former Joys
   On Saturday Afternoons in 1963 - Rickie Lee Jones
Walk-About
   Bright Lights and City Scapes - Sara Bareilles
The Ink of Every Inkling
   Wonderful Unknown - Ingrid Michaelson
Presenting the Past
   Breakable - Ingrid Michaelson
This the Latest
   Between the Lines - Sara Bareilles
Corpus Delicate
   Islands - Sara Bareilles
View without You, View without Hue
   Here Comes the Flood - Peter Gabriel
Simple Steps and Their Adumbrations
   Breathe Again - Sara Bareilles
Stolen, Even Stolen Looks
   Washing of the Water - Peter Gabriel
A Thousand Pictures for a Word
   Once Upon Another Time - Sara Bareilles
Bridging Blankness
   Everyone is Gonna Love Me (demo) - Ingrid Michaelson
Touchstone
   Over You (demo) - Ingrid Michaelson
Good-Bye is So Long
   O - Coldplay
Not Just Her Story
   Old Days - Ingrid Michaelson
The Dissolution of Days
   Satellite Call - Sara Bareilles
Abandonment Not Meant
   I Remember Her - Ingrid Michaelson
Ill Logic, All
   Open Hands - Ingrid Michaelson
Kepplerian Epicycles
   Turn to Stone - Ingrid Michaelson
Gifting the Gap
   Everglow - Cold Play
Boxes
   Ready to Lose - Ingrid Michaelson

Table of Contents

in memory
of that

Preface

It started with - and for the longest time remained - a single symptom; repeating questions which had just been answered; incapacitation's precursor - inconvenience. Official diagnosis finally came in 2009, but clinical assessment was a formality, since at that point my mother had been (in hindsight) in decline for nearly a decade.

For as long as possible, we'd held out hope for reversible/ surmountable causes: delayed and particularly vicious aftershocks of menopause; the temporary imbalancings of changes in life's circumstance (my dad's retirement, diminished call for her own professional activities as an archaeologist, the arrival of grandchildren and their unintended reminder of mortality); depression over her father's death, and the decline of an extended family's matriarch in her late nineties - her own and always extremely capable mother.

But new normals brought no return of previous faculties. Just the opposite. Amended baselines put further fallings off in stark relief: the subtle flattening of feeling and expression; slow evaporation of the executive function (the forgetting of processes and the purpose of implements); and an unmaking of the interactive (the failing of speech, then visible comprehension, and gradual inanimation).

My father, a dedicated hiker, once described 'lost' as something you find yourself to be - not becoming; the realization belatedly following the reality; a harrowing which lacks the mitigation of a harbinger.

That departure from the norm mirrors the strangeness of succumbing by Alzheimer's, the suspension of the routine which - absent such afflictions - we're unlikely to view decline and death as...

...the surprisingly unsettling symmetry, a life ebbing out of existence as gradually as it flowed in; sentence without punctuation, the final robbed of its accustomed finality.   (The waveform of a life is expected to propagate anti-parallel to that of its soundtrack (speech), realized when we see existence not playing out as a record run backward.)

...the reversal of one mate's status - from adult to child, coupled with the looping of the other's role - from partner to parent to simply partner to suddenly parent again...

...the inversion of the suffering spectrum; the afflicted growing less pained as they grow more affected...

...and the doubling of that phenomenon; the resonances of the witnessing amplified as the diseased's distress becomes more muted (maybe more accurately, the shifting of the burden - suffering's abandonment by one being taken up by the other, as suffering's surrogate)...

...the general unsyncing of self and substance, the losing before the taking leave, the body and its needs remaining after the person has fled, and our especial haunting by that ghosting-in-reverse (the changeling substitution of substance sans spirit for the somehow less untoward of spirit sans substance); our insistence on treating the one present as the one past - that preservation providing sole solace.

The following aren't attempts to explain these Moebius matters, to iron the wrinkles satisfyingly flat or offer prescriptions, simply observations and emotings, attempt at kenning in the keening. Words must out, and since mine can no longer be with, or assuredly to... now only of and for. I don't share them with the illusion of assuaging, merely hope of commiserating. But in commiseration, maybe a semblance of comfort for others travelling the same path; some small assurance, as they grow ever more alone, that they are not alone.

And despite the tone, not to be taken as dirge, but goad - encouragement to do likewise; to commemorate significant lives while engaging in the therapeutic of a purgative, an emetic (poemetics perhaps), excising the sad so that which tends to choke can be got out and their own lives continued, renewing focus on animation and efforts to make the most of today, given that tomorrows aren't promised. And in doing so, honor those who so ably exemplified appreciation of that fact.

- January 2018

Sorrow is Shadow　Cast by Former Joys

The Minnequa say,
"The soul would have no rainbow　if the eyes had no tears."
only the heavy heart　a full heart

Some leave before their losing　but remain well past passing.
I like　and need
to think　and hope
latter retards former　as former fosters latter.

not the losing,　the having had...
not the losing,　the having had...

And to the towering pile　of all these inversions,
that one alone　willingly thrown on;
child Grief　birthing parent Joy.

Thus hoped these words　not heard
a lamentation's wail,　rather seen portrait of a love,
albeit reflected in　the mirror of missing.

- 29 Nov 2016

Oh, for Damnatio Memoriae, Its Own Fate

For the longest time
we banned its name
from even
vestibule of thought,
refusing to entertain
possibility that the
shadow's footprints
might imply
The Absenting's
presence.

For a longer time
we were unsure
reticence's reason:
if from unease
that the calling
might prove a conjuring,
phantom made fact,
allowed if aloud…
or embarrassment
in mere vincibility;
chary that a body's
betrayal of itself
somehow showed
a deservedness,
as though a failing
connoted a failure.

But for a good while now -
fright having given way
to frustration
(anger revealed
impotent in its charge
to effect change) -
we've known
better reason:
to be loath to dignify
The Undignifying with
least acknowledgement;
resentful of ceding voice
to The Thief of Tongues;
reluctant to gift
The Taker of Names
one more
unwarranted trophy...
knowing our
hurling of epithets
in the face of epitaphs
reveals us captives of an
unpardoning confusion,
but preferring that to
conceding least sense
pretended by
The Senseless.

- 07 Dec 2016

Journal Entry: 10 Jun 2009

With all my world sleeping, here in the home of my wife's parents, wakeful hours lead me to that of my own, and the unexpected turn their path is taking.

My Mother's gentle unbecoming, the unravelling, the erasing of what was once an appreciably full page, becomes less deniable with every discrete (discontinuous, unequivocal) shift. The latest is Dad's decision to put Mom in, well, adult daycare for three days a week. To find a few hours not wholly in the attending of another, a respite from focus fully external, to the exclusion of self.

A hard decision for him to make I'm sure, *despite* meeting the needs of both (*since* meeting the needs of <u>both</u>). A conscience will niggle with the afforded second-guessing of whose was put primary and whether the resolution had purity therefore.

Because it would be hard, even for a husband, not to be resentful of circumstances when potential is truncated, the entertained future of finding/bestowing enjoyment in/on another dimmed as the result of that one - no matter the other incapable of effecting that end or any otherwise.

And harder still to evade greater guilt of having, in human moments, not *not* blamed the blameless, accused those incapable of defending their innocence even if they weren't already beleaguered by cold happenstance.

I hope, during the primary parent years, Dad didn't sustain himself on consideration of reward of eventual return to (even more) carefree coupledom, as that'd be a mean fate braying at a proud man; most abrupt end to that anticipated Eden; affording the least amount of time possible to reconcile one's self to a prior phase of life irrevocably (and unconsentingly, because unforeseeably) laid aside on entering into family in fullest sense, dooming one to unwitting under-appreciation of days not then known to be already at their fullest on *all* fronts (the whole optimized though no single aspect maximized).

I wish I had certitude of the "things within/beyond control" demarcation line, to know if what I'm doing in Dad's regard is enabling or offering rightly placed affirmations (albeit out-of-place, so maybe just ersatz). I'm sure I'm wrestling him for wanting ownership of that certitude, that it's a cause of his insomnia.

Beyond that, I hate that the all of my energies are to empathizing with him, the most aware so presumably most acutely pained, with none reserved, even as leftovers, for Mom, likely less pained but likely more frightened, and with less and ever less time to be recipient of what salve such regard might prove, if only provided.

As to why that is, I'm afraid my orientation might be more toward getting consolation (the golden panacea of some arcane sorting out of all this) rather than giving comfort, and *that*, pathetically, is me putting me at the center of this.

I don't know if I'm holding out for some over-the-next-hill moment of "being able to do the most for" which will come only with full appreciation of the primary and secondary impacts on everyone. Might as well make the appointment for getting in gear at such time as the backside of the rainbow comes into view. You can't get there from here, and if the 'where' of destination requires that imaginary point as way stop, doesn't this all become clutched excuse to wander in the wilderness and not arrive in(/at any) time?

Walk-About

My Mother
left on walk-about Saturday,
opened the door into fall
and ambled up the path to
hill's top.

Around a neighbor's house
for good measure
then down the other side,
letting gravity carry her
where it would
and has for so long
it seems.

It had her steps moving along
streets she'd never;
corners merely glimpsed -
forborne by twenty-six years'
purposeful journeying
that neighborhood -
now allowed the full focus
of unfocus.

Meanwhile, home,
my father left alone,
not knowing how long,
knew the rise of fright
which is the flight of order.

On Saturday
My Mother tottered off
as once when a child of four.
Maybe in search of that time
and the new magic of motion,
or to cover, re-cover, recover
the distance years
somehow insinuated
between her and her
when days weren't
at their watching.

Dogs went tracking
and police eventually
brought back what they could
of My Mother
to once again sit in her chair
and think the thoughts
which are hers alone.

And maybe consider
next outing,
to explore the
surely enticing
ever wider worlds
opening before her.

We put latches on doors,
beyond the stretching of hands,
and wish memory, longing,
regard, grief - any,
could forge bolts
strong enough
to bar real leaving,
but she goes where she will
and we all wouldn't.

To places dimly glimpsed
so dimly viewed,
and maybe not even objected
so much the going
as the going alone,
and leaving likewise;
those who have the time
to still go anywhere
and those whom time affords
the luxury to go nowhere
finding themselves
surprisingly at juncture,
(on reflection shown anticable)
in remembrance that such
ever indicates crossroads.

- 22 Dec 2011

The Ink of Every Inkling

Speaking volumes,
they say
when a person dies
a library burns.
And we the witnessing
begin to imagine
smoke in the wind.

My Mother has long
made of her mind
a page full
to over-flowing
with a life's
neatly scribed,
hard-won lines.
Of queries, verities,
entreaties, beauties;
sentiences of sentences &
exclamations of wonder.
A folio sheet
carefully folded
to prevent those pennings'
slide off the bottom
(and again)
to stop them
running out the side
(and again)
to make pocketable,
keep close to heart,
impress the importance
of that parchment.

Equally,
the matter of the metaphor
there behind her eyes...
Nestled in the lee
of those crenellating folds
lie untold chemical squiggles,
held fast by
a sky's stars'
number of neurons;
the myriad of moments
which amalgam
constitutes a being
and a having been.

Until now,
as the anti-poetic
of a ripping tide
of amyloid plaques
and tau tangles
begins to wash over all,
loosing and losing,
scraping those coves clean
with the surety
of a curettage,
leaving no purchase
for all thus bought;
stores painstakingly laid up
slipping unceasingly away,
to dissipation
and desperation.

That is epilogue
to the book of her,
becoming all too open
as entropy's questing
and clumsy hands
pry apart her sheets' folds,
spilling truths,
scattering selves,
pressing and smoothing
the page of a presence
again as flat and uncradling
as a bloom in an
un-memory book;
reconstituting the ink
of every inkling
which - liquid again -
is drawn from
once-slaked fibers,
all to dribble away
and there be
inscribed no more.

Once I read a short story
in which each of the many
names of God was recited
in order to usher
the end of times,
resulting in all the
coruscating points
in the heavens
slowly winking out.
We would do the same,
that this same not.

- Jul 2009

A Loan for Alone

My parents always said,
"Neither a borrower
nor a lender be"
not stood on by or
standing on another.
Live within
your means,
no matter how
mean and tempting.
Yet here we are...
buying grief
on the installment plan,
its cost too great
to be settled
lump sum
regardless how much
capital tucked away;
upside down in
all these reversals,
attempting to secure
a situation which
affords no purchase;
paying interest
on that
which holds
less than none,
accounting for
seeing so much red
in the midst of
so much black;
wondering,
that 'equity' would
even be a word.

- 08 Feb 2017

My Mother's Gentle Unbecoming

My Mother's unbecoming
has not been unbecoming,
and we thank heaven
for that small favor.
Others' is.
Some tattoo
Mr. Thomas' words
to their days,
going not quietly into
their early night,
raging against
the dying of their light,
flailing at
fear and frustration,
cutting the air
and all in witness.

But she,
becoming again
child-like,
looks to all with
that soft openness,
pantomiming the
many quiets
which will
ultimately envelope,
her poise in
the face of
the insurmountable
unaccountable.
Leaving us
to wonder
if her retention
of equanimity
is fortune's
last gift to her,
or hers to us.
Her holding
of her nature
is balm to both,
but preserving
our feeling,
it pains
our good-byes
all the more.

Causing question
if God demands
parity to the person,
that all lives
average out,
each a balanced
equation in which
everything cancels.
Is keen discernment
inextricably linked
to inevitable opposite,
perspicuity tied
Gordian to this
descending fog,
a balloon moored
to millstone?
Does daring flight
demand a fall,
or simply make
the coming to ground
more marked for those
who aspired heights?

Others also speak of opposites.
I think of Messr. Eliot,
and his wondering
at the way worlds end,
believing and hoping
him false in his dilemma;
the passing of such
not proceeding with a whimper
or a bang, but a whisper,
as of a breeze's last exhalation
through an open window.
Finding -
in the absence of a shout's
abrupt ceasing -
promise of a quiescence's
echo on to beyond,
not in the least diminished...
simply dimmed
to the seeing
of this side.

- May 2010

02 May 2011

Dad,

I wish I had words for this, other than to parrot the three heading your e-mail - A Gloomy Portent, which do a regrettably good job of capturing things.

I don't know which is more cruel, the ravaging of the mind or the body. The former, defining, is more personal. The latter, fundamental, seems more vicious. And given the facility of the mind, the ebb and flo its progression takes, bad days can be chased by good ones, allowing anticipation of rescission, reprieves from the slide. When the physical begins its decline, I don't know if that's the death of hope or the arrival of acceptance.

I hate to think the two synonymous. But then I'd hate to think either would ever occur. None of us has to acquiesce to any of this.

Comes a time, maybe, when all we own is our attitude toward such circumscribing circumstances. And maybe the last and least we can give, to those who've gone beyond the ability to mold their feelings as they would, is to couch ours in the best way, in hopes the empathic holds and they can enjoy a bit longer than otherwise; the carrying of the vicarious.

Stay strong. I'd imagine it's a curse to be able to, suffering the temptation to surrender which the option brings, a deliberation folks of less fortitude are spared.

But if you feel like a moment loose, the attached might aid the unknotting. It's by Sara Bareilles, the artist Jim and I saw in Asheville two weeks ago.

Thinking of you, thinking of her, thinking.

All my not enough love,
Dan

By One's Self, By One's Own Hand

A book I've been
meaning to read
(on a single paragraph's
recommendation)
has soldiers in
an Eastern theater
agreeing to be
water-boarded
by one another,
in hopes of gaining
some empathy for
(perhaps offering
small penance to)
those they suffer
the same.

The author's curiosity:
at the moment
when drowning
feels imminent,
when it seems
one's fellows
have gone farther
than agreed
(or imagined),
which fear will
shriek foremost -
that of having been
Misunderstood
or Betrayed.

I see you there,
struggling to return,
in your eyes
again the question
if this the time
truly past the last,
fully beyond
re-scaling the
paling fence,
and suspect
your fate
worse than any
character's fiction:
the horror of
either reality
at one's own hand
(Unintelligibility
or Abandonment)
far exceeding both
at any other's.

So why the
exercise in torture
of contemplating the self
both object and subject,
the doubling of pain
in the halving
of principals?

In hopes to avert:
that if the whole
dissected,
full effect splayed
and laid bare
for the cosmos
to look upon,
none
would prove so dark
as to not turn away
from perpetrating such.

Or if so,
at least to blunt the searing,
to have found inoculation
from that inconsiderable
in lesser pain
of the mere
near unbearable.

- 30 Dec 2016

Presenting the Past

Her professional passion
was to find the lost,
excavate the peoples
of forgotten time,
reconstructing the bits,
the broken, the buried,
returning them to a
semblance of life,
and gifting us
a measure
in the process;
our seeing in full
of who we are
in how we were.

Now on dusty shelves
rest the implements
of her hands'
long embrace,
measuring tape, note pad,
stadia rod & plumb line,
trowel & brush,
still telling with
earth's grime.
And were I
at the ready
to take them up,
better pupil of parent,
able to track her path,
I'd have this all
by more than half.

Then again,
that I don't
is maybe
truer tribute
than realized,
the function of
the archaeologist
being only
to recover,
her sister
the anthropologist's -
to animate;
the one just to
make aware the past,
the other to breathe
intimate the present,
and none's - it seems -
to effect a trading
between those verbs
and their objects.

And so times sit
upon their walls,
gently rocking,
and all the
king's horses
and the damned
king's men…

- 28 Aug 2015

Dad,

...I'm not surprised about Mom. Even as distant as I am, with so few data points to plot, I can tell her abilities with thought are dwindling. The last two times I've called, she's suddenly diverted to reading me passages from books at hand. The will remains, the momentum that is the spark; where her words escape, she substitutes others'. It's touching & too sad. And it makes me glad awareness can't follow where such things go. That'd be cruelest cut yet.

Some days it makes me frantic, wondering if heredity will gift me the same as her and her father & aunt before her. Words are the things I've prided myself on most through my life, that microscope of the mind which brings into focus such minutiae and delineates subtly distinct, otherwise confused, ill-discerned thought. And while losing them wouldn't be to have lost all (sensation would remain awhile), absent the amplification which reflection provides, the experiences of life would lose the full appreciation they're due, and I'd hate to become such a poor, ungrateful audience to the world's wonders.

Knowing, or even just suspecting the number of days allotted probably has different effects on different folks, depending on the person and point in the journey at which it comes. For me, it drives vacillation between wanting to sit infinitely still, to absorb the immensity every moment can muster, and frenetic scurrying to fill them all with impossible significance. If eighteen years are all I have left to call my own, cognitively continent, I'm well behind where I need to be in making marks and - as Horace Mann charged - avoiding the shame of dying before I've achieved some small victory for humanity (via words I would cobble into patterns to please the mind's eye and inspire others likewise), though appreciating - and appreciating, if experience is indicator - that greatest impact will be elsewhere and somewhat accidental, as husband and father. If I will be becoming lost to my boys before they're three-fourth's my young age, if the clock has spent half its unrelenting play, I need to play so much more and faster.

And hope my preoccupations aren't a pall on their days. I'd hope they can't put two and two together or entertain a consequence. But, I'd hate more if they couldn't. Gifts cost that way. Just don't want to suck oxygen from rooms and taint *their* time, have them growing up preternaturally sad, the joy in the new and burgeoning leached by too frequent glances to possibilities possibly looming and the sad example of their dad giving up on days before their due.

And again, this is me failing to look beyond myself. I hope I don't shame myself in your eyes by failing to focus on the one for whom the opportunity to care is briefest. I tell myself the failing is partly one of the words to dress the thoughts adequately, trying to reconcile the vitality - in bookcases overflowing with letters, diaries, research papers, theses, reports and archives, photos of so many occasions mischievous and playful and pensive, more vibrant still than the Kodachrome hues in which they're captured, all the myriad trappings and static, resounding echoes of a life laid out, the vigor which brought them all into being and inspired awe and desire to emulate such energies - trying to reconcile that vitality with its absence. For such a constant force to be rendered otherwise... that defiance of physics, experience and desire doesn't lend itself to grasping.

Know that you're both in all our thoughts. Times like these I envy your daughter-in-law. Someone said men's communication is centered on solving problems and women's on empathizing. While not all problems have solutions, all circumstances can be met with fellow-feeling. Hers has greater application. Maybe at end this all just calls for less frustration-at and more feeling-for.

Love and regards,
Dan

This the Latest

Books...

Once upon a time
devoured by My Mother.
First by newly cut teeth,
exploring a taste
not yet cultivated.
Then a searching mind's
ravening appetite,
on which it grew ponderous.

But too soon they
became locked stores
of strange incantations,
hieroglyphs sussurated
under the attent of bifocals
in search of the magic
inexplicably concealed;
spells once held
which timbre, meter and accent
had escaped.

Sometime later,
when even
phonemes failed,
the search gave over
to hieroglyphs
of her own;
under-scoring each passage
in wavering pencil,
asserting
in imitation
the impossibly equal
importance of them all.

And all too recently
the rendering
has returned to rending,
just the -scoring;
endless cutting with shears
along the irregularly dotted lines
of other's making
in effort to
excise the elusive -
the essence
seemingly somehow
still within the thin planes
of those confounding pages.
Not discovered pressed between
them or their lines,
the search has expanded
to the interstices
of all the nothings
which alone now
present themselves
for review and revisiting.

Sometimes she shivers
in the snow of those slivers
mounding 'round her chair,
perhaps sensing the coldness
in the melting of meaning.
But she presses on.

And I applaud and weep the labor,
praising the drive
while rueing the direction,
and the collusion of those two,
each by the other
made commentator,
backlighting in stark relief
the will which yet abides
when the way has fled
and so can no longer find a path
to any home,
despite that being
the thing
a will fashioned for.

- Jul 2010

Corpus Delicate

What's etiquette's edict
when two are in a room
and one departs,
but only to
the other's seeing?
Slip out likewise?
Pretend the one still there?
Wait for the return
which will never come?

I cry a crime,
yet others hear only wolf,
calling premature the charge,
citing juris' prudence -
intended insurance
against wrongful suit:
"Corpus delecti -
body of evidence:
(foremost among,
that of a
purported victim;
substance sans spirit)!
How a wrongful death,
when the alleged's extant?"

But real affront
is that protection's
complicating of
this one's prosecution,
the absence of evidence
assumed in the evident:
the only case
more difficult to plead
than murder without a body...
such a taking
in the presence of one.

This the shadow statute
given short shrift,
the less reconcilable
so more egregious
Corpus delicate -
substance sans spirit
of any substance;
the uneasy attempt
to account for the form
which animation's
inertial only.

Thus a mistrial declared
in the trials
of the missing,
in pleas for pardon
of the victim;
case dismissed,
whistled past,
plaintive plaintiffs
left alone in these
cavernous halls
of 'just us'.

So please, tell me, Judge
in your wizened ways,
how best to plot
these trackless days?
Who, beyond refute,
to prosecute?
What, for this offense,
just recompense?

- 28 Aug 2015

View without You, View without Hue

Despair is well
which won't run dry.
No matter how much
that draught we quaff,
drown-able depths remain
(for all but Anguish...
that sinking
alone unsinkable).

Grief is river
unlike any other,
of which Absence
is greatest tributary
and to which
the bereaved
all run
as tributaries;
a rushing current
from which
one never once
steps past passed
to be beyond.

Frustration is ocean
un-navigable
by any sextant extant,
untracked no matter
how often plied;
even far stars'
guiding fires
extinguished in
its expanses,
mind unmoored
by the seemingly
unshored.

Woe's water is
medium only by half
(hoped necromancy,
mere fancy)
but *against* hope, hale -
conveying even greatest
to lowest ground:
life-drowning
death-quenching
draught of naught,
the reign of
the rain of ruin,
which falls
not *just* -
just on and on
unliked.

- 19 Sep 2016

Simple Steps and Their Adumbrations

Today My Mother
crossed the threshold
of her home
the final time
and knew it not.
We all did on her behalf
and wished that could balance,
lending her the significance
it should hold.

But her grasp is past,
there are no lasts
where no nexts await,
and hers has become
a fixed present;
a record riding
the same groove interminably,
losing the skip only when
the needling has dug
below the sound;
film caught in endless loop,
marionetting motion back
again and again
until called perfected
in the emulsion's running;
the anything-but-suspended sentence
of a life in unending suspension,
completed
as some are
in incompletion.

I wonder if this day
my father thought back
to first crossing,
the other direction,
and staggered under
the felling ache
for that distant day's
buoyant wonder
at all those ahead,
luminous and innumerable.

For My Mother
it is mirroring moment...
carried this time
in the arms of un-remembrance,
the infinity she embraces
borne of un-iteration.

We the witnessing
wish we could be spirited so,
enjoying her ignorance
of when each chapter will end
as compensation
for our knowing how;
that her fate (if it be such)
at least be shared,
as was all else in a life.

But fate refuses small favors,
leaving us to envy
those who now suffer
only by our proxy.
And not having learned
that 'last' and 'lasting' lie
when they tout themselves
any way relations,
we gather up
each falling moment
like the pieces of
a prized china plate.
We hold, we count them all,
trying to see what was
in what isn't,
and wish *ourselves*
insensible.

Last seat at this table,
 last hand on this glass,
  last holding of this cat,
   last look out this window,
    last laugh in these walls,
     last tread on this stair,
      last cheek on this pillow,
       last night beneath this roof,
        last lying next to this man,
         last dawn creeping in,
          last turn of this latch,
           last push of this door,
            last gaze on this lawn...

- 02 Sep 2012

Beneath the Fool's Cap

Monday at a lunch headed by
3rd Air Force's latest
(Lieutenant General Franklin)
here at Incirlik AB, Turkey
for first meet-and-greet,
and me part of the feeding furniture
in the Istanbul Room
of the Consolidated Club.

Neighbor to the left
intractably in conversation with his,
I turn to my other -
the scenery beyond table's end;
non-descript wall and its door
to all which awaits
in a week ever burgeoning.

The handle of that is singular -
twisted angle iron, silvered and thick.
I imagine the work that went into
its arabesqueing
and try to run the process backward,
discern - given the leverage afforded
and required of the smith -
the order of the untwisting of the bar.
and, if still affixed to its
raison d'être by one leg,
uncontorting like some Japanese
paper flower done up in stainless,
what the appearance
at each stepping back:
which part, still parallel
to door's plane,
would stand as the pull at that point.

And, if introducing
an employing arm
into the equation,
what point of attachment
and orientation it would take
(thus hopefully conveying
entire consideration wordlessly
to any other,
equally attenting).

That done, and
the moment still not at end,
consideration bleeds outward
searching the connection
between the pair of nature prints
framing said portal.
Each boasts three aspen
foregrounding a pond
fronting red barn and residence,
the latter frothed in
high summer wheat...
the trees in this one,
if walked to the right
three paces,
become - I believe -
the trees in that.
Hypothesis confirmed
in the direction and degree
of the house's migration
relative to the boles
with such plotted movement.

Then, for completeness' sake,
test the order
of the two
in their hanging
by their rotating unfolding;
if left hand truly represents
left-hand view
to an orbitting observer,
or if the effect's achievable
only by insinuating
the split scene
(now necessarily transparent
save in reflection)
between self and
a posited mirror.

These the places
a mind goes
when impatient
for a body
to take it some (any) other.
Or,
maybe where
taken (hostage)
when a body's
desperate to be
freed from
a moment
bereft
momentum.

And given the taxing
of such diversions,
I can't help but wonder
if after a while,
mind,
tired of being driven
to places so far beyond
the reasonably expected,
simply decides to
take its leave,
accommodating body's
unwitting wish
to be relieved
its awareness
of its surroundings,
in unrealized,
unbidden fullness;
if that is how these
endings
- so much in my
thoughts lately -
ultimately begin.

And if, knowing that,
I could,
        would
bend myself to unmaking
the snare of such
cognitive cat's cradle
and possibly
have a hope
of beginning *their* ending.

- 16 Apr 2012

Stolen, Even Stolen Looks

My mother
walks naked
through her days,
unembarrassed
only because
unknowing.
Fully clothed
but fully unclosed,
revealing to all
who happen by
the bits
she would have
every day but
this unending last
kept hidden.
The private
she alone
should possess,
stolen and paraded
by an oblivion
which has
her unseeing
her seeing,
and so un-allowed,
the concealing
of the concerning.

Having left,
she is the voyager.
Left gazing after,
we are the voyeurs.
Even our
last looks,
lost looks;
heavily mantled,
garbed in guilt
for their theft
of consideration's
consent.

I wish I could
be the good boy,
cover the
bareness of
her barrenness;
once be for she
as she once for me.
But that would be
to look away,
and that
maybe in end
more cut
than courtesy.

- 09 Aug 2016

A Thousand Pictures for a Word

Now I know
why My Mother said
don't run with scissors,
having witnessed
her long-delayed
demonstration
of the consequences.

Where just moments ago
neat stacks of
glossy squares
sat sorted,
now lies a litter of leaves
in full fall color,
two dozen family snapshots
origami-ed into abstraction,
disembackgrounded bodies
haloed by broken borders:
most of them
perfectly cropped
baby pictures,
the earliest evidence of
herself with her eldest.

She has separated
the then-so-recently met
(and so recently re-found),
perhaps taking cue from
the inevitable inherent therein;
seeking to echo the individuation
which has been replaying
in every other association,
or perhaps in a desperate bid
to undo all the undoings,
last back to first.

I, contrary by her nature,
pursue another path,
working instead
to stitch things together.
I look for meaning in meanderings
imagine paths in voids,
and won't not wonder
at every insignificant aspect,
trying to compute
what I can't refute.

Whether this all
has been a cutting out
or a cutting away;
absenting the essential
(no longer such)
or removing the dross
to keep in focus
the hard held
former images
of current shards.

Maybe this is letting go
and saying good-bye.
Maybe this is nothing,
last good-byes
having echoed out
before our ears could hear.

And last quandary,
which always overstays
its hour on stage...
"Between those poles
- assigning,
          resigning -
which is better,
and which worse?"

Dread tells me
that the worst
is to get it wrong.
and I know
that to be true,
because I know
I cannot but...
the answer
to both
being "Both".

   - 16 Apr 2011

Bridging Blankness

Following a formality
pretexted breakfast,
I sit a moment
with My Mother
in her room.
And since my words alone
echo too loudly
we substitute the wordless.
And holding hands
I realize her wedding bands
have gone missing,
here in this place
where none
retain anything.

As she falls into sleep,
freed the shackles
of consciousness'
complexities,
she twitches, at last
returning my grasp,
and I smile at the jibe;
her unintended communication
so perfectly mimocking
my transmissions in the blind.

And while as likely
she hasn't heard
what I've said
as it is that I have
what she hasn't,
since imagination's
yet allowed
I remind myself
the core functions
abide longest,
and insist
we're not chasing ghosts
but exercising
the elemental.
No one protests,
and if silence
can be acquiescence,
maybe artifice
can be accomplice.
At least a moment more.

- 03 Jan 2014

Touchstone

Most of the few
things I've broken
have been in anger.
This should have
been the same,
(though more justified
than the rest).
But it wasn't.
Instead,
the crooked grin
now spreading
across the otherwise
pristine and polished
face of my iMac's
wireless mouse
was induced
by accident.
Dropped,
concussed on keyboard
while selecting
soundtrack
to compose
yet another silent call
to my mom.

When we grope
in unfamiliar places
nothing feels right
or even at all.
When we move
in unfamiliar ways,
we work without
the net of reflexes
and innocents
fall prey to our
clumsy clutching.

And as if reminder
more were needed
for that which -
like a burned retina -
is ever before me,
touchstone is now
always at my fingertip,
telling...
at my every attempt
at turning
from.

- 01 Apr 2014

Good-Bye is So Long

At the arrival
of all departures,
a ritual in my
maternal family
is to gather curbside
and wave vigorously
until the leaving
have exceeded sight,
as though to generate
a following breeze
to carry them
their distance.

Doubtless before done,
the receding's eyes
have moved wholly
to their homing,
so those seeing off
might feel
just a bit silly.

But having sat
that moving seat,
looked back at limit
(just to see *if*...
assure *that*...)
I know at far end
the tether is hoped and held
as long as held forth,
that arms bear
beyond their grasp,
well past the point
clouded or dimmed
eyes can discern
if those motions
a beckoning or sending,
the leaving's comfort
compounded by ambiguity's
doubling of the hastening;
knowing they go
with both
-breaking and blessing,
swaddled
(in that embrace
and that release)
by love's fraternal twins;
the hoped of
and hoped for.

- 07 Dec 2016

Not Just Her Story

I sit in this creaky wooden chair,
bearing a decal branding it
property of Texas A & M College,
transcribing words
from pages of onion skin
tattooed with carbon paper shadows,
of events of days
before I was a glimmer,
shifting them to a virtual sheet
of contrasting photons,
knowing as I spend mornings
stitching together these technologies,
I do so in the same seat
from which My Mother
first chronicled that life in ascent;
my mind and my eyes
occupying the same spaces
as hers a half century ago.

And all that I want,
beyond remembering
events I've forgotten,
is to eliminate last least gap;
have this glass plate
of a platen before me
become more perfect mirror,
so the reflection
of my reflections
on hers
might put her again here before me
in sight and consideration -
pulling me back into
times and conditions I would,
rather than behind -
pushing me on
to places I'd not.

But hindsight remains 20/200,
making this alone clear...
The connection which
history at five or six
heartbeats' remove holds
is at most
the least;
that commonest denominator -
the human condition;
only the leavings of
his story or hers.

One's own,
held within adjoining
generations' arc
(no matter the years' span)
isn't.
Not history,
just an unsettlingly
un-solid present,
somehow
somewhat misplaced,
so steadfastly
wanting finding.

- 17 Mar 2014

The Dissolution of Days

I remember when...
I stood in the middle
of my room
at night
in the dark
and cried,
because My Mother
wasn't there
and wasn't coming.

The next morning
I awoke,
and wrote
these words.

And wondered...
that it's not just
one's own last days
which recall one's first.

And wondered more...
if we can
be reduced
to former states,
why can't we
be returned
to them?

      - 10 Apr 2014

Abandonment Not Meant

These days
I'm saddest
because surprised
at remembering
My Mother is
still alive.
Like waking
to realize
the bad
was just a dream
- in reverse.

No longer
in any place
of shared sojourn,
association
has dwindled
to recollection -
domain of the departed,
and I'm shamed
by the failing,
having buried
before her passing
the one who kept
vigil over me
before even I was.

I, who once gloried
in youth's burgeoning,
proven so much
the weaker;
she having held
more tightly
by briefest gaze
and merest touch
than I
in powerful arms
and plumbless memory.

It's hard to watch
your mother die.
Harder still
to watch her not.
Hard to see yourself
watching the clock
and ever again dare
a mirror's approach.

- Jul 2013

Ill Logic, All

If life the wares
and death the price,
and we given
to anthropomorphizing
the metamorphosis,
and uncharitably seeing
it seeing likewise -
for a species
of stretching spans,
this epidemic
of enfeeblement
could be construed
death's cheating of those
who would cheat it.

But to what end,
projecting the human
on the inhumane...
To allay? To alloy?
To clothe the alien
in the familiar
of the familial?
To paste a face
on enigma frustration?
To cancel the bitter
of the unintelligible
by the sweet
of the kindred?
To drag it down
to the realm
of the forgiveable?

All being academic,
none make the grade.

In an irony
pronounced ignominy
My Mother's stock
is particularly long-lived,
creating my father's
dread of pre-deceasing;
what (pre-diagnosis)
was likely
a private comfort,
now a personal fear.

Of failing his duty
to provide for her,
or - at the least - to
remain her consideration,
staving off
injury's insulting...
that the unremembering
not become
the unremembered;
the now unknowing
still known;
that full demise
not break ranks
and outrun death.

His full failure -
the clock's failing
of him,
ushering in the worst
of both worlds.
So he works steadily
to extend his allotted,
to live more
to live for,
and avoid Horus
painting him
both the abandoned
and the abandoner.

Strange math it is,
that we take up
the buoyant burden
of carrying others
on paths they
can no longer
traverse alone,
holding them in
attentions' untiring arms,
while they carry
bits of us away with
their receding tidings.

What it is,
the wearing of
the wearing of
these wares...

- 20 Aug 2015

Kepplerian Epicycles

Her eyes are wary as
mine peer around her door,
until the slow of
my motions and
quiet in my tone
assure no threat.
I don't take it personally,
knowing fear lies
not so much in things
as their unfamiliarity.
Realizing only later
it properly personal -
her look merely
mirroring mine.

As we sit, I gaze on a
visage once my moon -
ethereal, encircling,
luminous above,
and see it again so -
distant, elliptic,
wan and one-faced.
Scanning that mask,
I seek the essence
behind the facade,
missing the deception
hiding in plain sight:
surface is only substance left.

This the way our
worlds go - ever away,
separating and thinning;
all things running
from center's collapse
- in fear or freedom -
to cohesion's fictioning,
the demise even of Nothing...

Substituting standing,
we pad down long halls,
pretending it to the world
beyond doors' windows' walls.
A lady falls into slipstream,
entreating, "Is it soon?"
and hopefully reassuringly
I answer, "Very soon."
Others are drawn
into our wake,
motes stitching a comet's tail
from agitation, aggregation,
the coincidence of
enough elapsings;
parents all
at gravity's birth.

Which gives me pause
and stupidest fancy -
remembering that
The Oscillating Theory
of the Universe
insists matter
stretches only to
momentum's farthest reach
before totality's tide reverses,
boomeranging back
into explosive unity;
the pendulemmings of the
sole perpetual motion machine
between singularity
and its greatest disparity.

In a moment's blindered jot
distance/proximity is all...
mere derivative of motion
strips the delta and its signs;
things coming or going
show the same.
And caught in the pull
of that straw's grasping,
nestling in that
ambiguity's expanse,
I fall to fever dream...

Maybe with sufficient
time and attendance,
what's gone awry
might come 'round again;
this apparent 'after'
prove at last
a burgeoning 'before'.

Son finds that sun -
warming, blinding tug
of improbable suspension
and sustainment...

All once thought, now lies ahead.
All once feared ahead - now lies.

I bask in that beacon
as we begin next circuit
and moth-like offer it homage
of our shuffling orbit.

- 19 May 2016

Journal Entry: 27 Oct 2016

I go to visit Mom this morning after breakfast. The access-granting administrator tells me if she isn't in her bedroom she might be in the common area for a birthday party. I head to her hall, remembering on opening door to empty walls that she now has a roommate, so go looking elsewhere. Just past the central corridor, I come to the new quarters - two beds but no one there. So off to the day room, where she asleep on a couch, looking like a left child, but otherwise well, her hair freshly done at the facility's beauty salon, nicely outfitted and peaceful. I pat her shoulder a few times, call her name, all to no effect, so let her sleep on, pretending it courtesy rather than quailing at thought of waking's return of realities.

Later, chocolate cake being served, I remember the new rules. Lack of demonstration isn't lack of want or need. I have to solicit the solicitation, so try rousing again to see if any interest on her part in partaking the occasion's material aspects.

Still no response to nudges or calling out, so I switch to 'Ruth', at which she instantly awakes. Not many calls for 'Mom' these days, and that not the name first or longest known by anyway, so it makes sense that incantation's now a lost one (though a personal sadness, it being the one which gave me my standing).

She looks around, and gravitating to me, it's only a moment before a shy, searching smile appears, which tugs in a way that takes me a minute to place. This is probably first look ever we shared, now reprised through traded eyes. I don't dwell on the difference, the anticipation then in hers for all the days ahead. In truth, there is no difference, as desire knows no demise, hope being impervious even to ineluctables.

Later, those who approach are viewed with apprehension, but looks to me remain open. I take that as a positive of what yet abides, locked within, but behind walls thankfully not yet opaque. Still capable of registering emotion, echoing awareness, expressing recognition, that transmission through seemingly insurmountable static affirms the ember of remember still glows.

Gifting the Gap

You showed me once
how much significance
can be gleaned from traces,
how much regained
from least remains:
witness carbon circles
in hard pack,
fixed shadows showing
ossified shells of
cells gone gangly -
footprint of a tree
repurposed center post.
And as a breadcrumb
prompts another's seeking,
the tattoo of those
connect-the-dots
discolorations in clay
outlines an edifice.

You demonstrate still,
as today we
placed ashes
in similarly
punctured earth,
it taking us three
to levy the weight
of your still presence.

Because if some
future archaeologist,
unaware the function
of cubed stones
cised with glyphs,
were to bare
your loamy blanket
they might be drawn
to similar conclusion,
in which they'd be
much wrong
but more right.

For you
were a dwelling,
a keep, a retreat, a haven,
a place of becoming,
burgeoning,
launchings and returns,
all you bore and bear
now turned prodigal
to what we knew not
but would not never;
turning earth
to turn days,
you to be borne,
we now to bear.

- 14 Nov 2017

Boxes

I. Vault

A treasure chest,
cribbed together
from dreams & days,
filled to spilling
with the richest
of feelings' fabrics...
At some point
closed and
hinges grown stiff,
then locked
and key full lost,
now sprung
and plundered -
any anticipation's
further allusion
exposed illusion.

II. Vessel

You
once home,
are house now;
empty rooms of
not enough expanse
for the pacings
of my gazes
on eyes
no more
to more
than mirror.

You
now home,
have been banished
to a room for one,
hastily and
clumsily cobbled,
too small
for the stores
of feeling
overflowing
its walls.

III. Vehicle

But maybe I mistake,
disparage out of hand.
Maybe there
unseen design -
reliquary not vessel
but vehicle;
crafted small to
size that welling
a deluge,
to prove buoyant
on its coursing,
this the only coach
capable of
carrying you
on to place
of next holding;
we still here
sheltered enough -
beholden
for being held
all ways and always.

IV. Volume

Book, too, is box,
built up of
thinnest boards,
the Volume
daring greatest
volume yet;
the Given
and the Riven
incongruously
stitched together
in the Graven,
pressed into
your hands
as you
into ours,
the codex seen
chameleon of
its brethren -
containing *and*
conveying.

Live here,
garmented in this
gathering of leaves,
identitied by
this sewing up
of signatures,
and so continue
your moving,
well beyond
this stuttering hand
and its feeble hold.

- 19 Dec 2017

Dan Wetmore spent his formative years in the halcyon hold of Laurinburg, N.C., where he earned a B.A. from Saint Andrews Presbyterian College in 1986, followed by an M.A. from Bowling Green State University, then parlayed dual degrees in Philosophy into a twenty-year career in the Air Force, including tours of duty on nuclear alert in a missile silo, as an instructor of Logic and Ethics at the Air Force Academy, launching satellites aboard decommissioned ICBMs, and overseeing a Communications Post in southern Turkey.

Having landed in Albuquerque N.M., he's now self-'employed', dividing days between the exploits of a wonderful wife and two enterprising sons, anchoring a chair at a local Starbucks under the pretense of writing, wrenching on various old cars, and hiking in the high desert mountains (but dreams of boomeranging back east to the land of green, seasons, and days past which seek to paint future ones).

Made in the USA
Columbia, SC
03 February 2019